Pennies from Heaven

Pennies from Heaven

By Kathleen Gunter

iv

ISBN 978-1-105-39385-3

DEDICATION

This book is dedicated to my Mom, Irene Abraham. She went home to the Lord in 2010, but left many legacies and many memories. She grew up during the pre-war years and the swing era. I learned all her music because she loved it and played it on the piano all the time. I was even named after a song, *I'll take you home again Kathleen*, so it's only appropriate this book be named after one of her favorite songs.

Pennies from Heaven.

Every time it rains, it rains
Pennies from Heaven
Don't you know each cloud contains
Pennies from Heaven

You'll find your fortunes falling
All over the town
Be sure that your umbrella
Is upside down

Trade them for a package of
Sunshine and flowers
If you want the things you love
You must have showers

So when you hear it thunder
Don't run under a tree
There'll be pennies from Heaven
For you and me

Trade them for a package of
Sunshine and flowers
If you want the things you love
You must have showers

So when you hear it thunder
Don't run under a tree
There'll be pennies from Heaven
For you and me

"Pennies from Heaven is a <u>1936</u> <u>American popular song</u> with music by <u>Arthur Johnston</u> and words by <u>Johnny Burke</u>. It was introduced by <u>Bing Crosby</u> in the 1936 <u>film of the same name</u>"

PREFACE

It seems that once we become Christians, we want to believe that only good things will happen to us and that only *blessings* will follow. Like spoiled children, we want to believe that God will miraculously deliver us from anything and everything bad; but, the longer we walk with Him, the more we understand, that tragic events happen even to believers. That doesn't make us bad nor does it imply that God does not love us. It simply means that by the grace of God, we do not walk through this life alone. The more we hurt, the more we need Him. Unfortunately, that's when we finally take time to listen for Him.

I like to write, although it seems to come in fits and starts. In the past, I've written for personal pleasure and for fun in *The Union Recorder*. I also wrote for an e-magazine, *Outreach*, (under the name, HisSong), Moselyville's newsletter: *The Mustard Seed*, *The Sandersville Progress*, and for *the 50's + Magazine* published by the *Union Recorder*.

Usually these were odd thoughts and observations. There's even some pretty bad poetry. (Sorry. We can't all be Sidney Lanier.)

I want to share these thoughts and observations and pieces of my life. So, this is a compilation of all those little ditties that I will call *Pennies from Heaven*.

TABLE OF CONTENTS

LORD I AM AFRAID

Lord,
You want me just as I am, but
What will I get in return?
Because I love you, I will give you My Blood as a covering
So that the terrors of hell cannot claim you.
I AM your Salvation.

Lord,
If I give you my life,
What will I get in return?
Because I love you, I will allow you to be persecuted
Until you realize that death is merely
The gateway to heaven.
I AM your reward.

Lord,
If I give you my heart,
What will I get in return?
Because I love you, I will give you a burden:
To love the unlovely,
To cry for the unwanted, and to grieve for the lost.
I AM the keeper of your heart.

Lord,
If I give you my pain,
What will I get in return?
Because I love you, I will allow you to hurt until
You can feel the suffering of others.
I AM your healer.

Lord,
If I give you my sorrow,
What will I get in return?
Because I love you, I will allow you to mourn until only I
can comfort you,
Then you will know why I am like Ramah crying for her
children who are no more.
I AM your comforter.

Lord,
If I give you my children,
What will I get in return?
Because I love you, I will give you my sword so that while
You are on your knees you will not be defenseless,
But strong against the powers that seek
To steal, kill, and destroy the innocent.
I AM your strength.

Lord,
If I give you my mate,
What will I get in return?
Because I love you, I will allow you to be tested to the very
Limits of your faith and your forgiveness.
I will teach you to persevere so that there may be healing.
I AM faithful and true.

Lord,
If I give you my unbelief,
What will I get in return?
Because I love you, I will allow you to fight the war of the
Believer that you may learn that even in defeat,
You are the victor, because I have already won.
I AM the author and finisher of your faith.

Lord,
If I give you my pride,
What will I get in return?

Because I love you, I will allow you to search out and
destroy every stronghold in your heart.
With tears of repentance you will wash
The feet of the brethren and sing my praises.
I AM the glory and the lifter of your head.

Lord,
If I give you my fears,
What will I get in return?
Because I love you, I will allow the winds to blow and the
Arrows to fly so that you will need Me to lead you
Through the days of darkness into my light.
I will never leave you or forsake you.
I am with you always.

Lord,
Now that I know, I am not afraid.

NEEDING TO BE NEEDED

It is nearly dark and I have many things left to do. My husband and three of the kids (son #3, daughters #2 and #3) are out picking the last of the blueberries. They wanted me to come out too, but I needed to wash the dishes and clean up the kitchen. It's the least I could do since my mother-in-law made the meat loaf for me tonight.

After washing dishes and cleaning the stove, I put my grandmother's clothes in to pre-soak before washing. They have got to be washed and dried tonight so I can take them to her at the nursing home tomorrow before we leave town. I should call our #2 son in Atlanta to make arrangements for tomorrow and get directions to his new house and our #1 son and his wife have not called me back yet. In a minute I will call my mom in Michigan to see what time her flight arrives Saturday. To top it off, I'm bothered by the puzzling message #1 daughter left earlier and I'm tickled #3 son dropped by tonight to economize and to EAT. Before I go to bed I need to set something out for tomorrow's supper and make some more iced tea. It's been a long day. My husband said we just might go to the DQ tonight after they've finished picking berries, but I should stay home. It is my turn to send something to Sal for *Outreach*. I had something planned, but somehow it doesn't seem to fit now.

My days aren't all like this, though they do get hectic as I get home from work. We still have the two youngest daughters living at home. The four oldest children have moved out. It's funny, for years I looked forward to the day when the children finally wouldn't need us anymore. I thought that would be when they hit 18 or when they went off to college. Each time it happened, I thought. "Ah, this is it!" But surprise! They still needed us.

They are typical children. Sometimes they need us for the obvious; MONEY!! Sometimes they need us for emotional support. Sometimes they need us to subconsciously remind them "who" they are and "how" they were raised. Not that we didn't make any mistakes. We have made plenty and those mistakes have come back to haunt us over and over again. Then there are the times they just enjoy our company. It feels great knowing they enjoy being with us.

It is interesting to note what I discovered; I'm not ready to be unneeded or unwanted. If I don't hear from them as often as I like, "I" end up calling them. It seems I just have to have my "kid" fix.

After all this, I guess it's obvious what I'm about to say. Perhaps this whole thought is for my benefit more than for yours. Our lives are so busy, so full, and so chaotic, yet our children still need us and take time to be with us, no matter how old they get or how far away they live. And we love to be here for them and look forward to those wonderful, noisy times.

Oh, Abba, now I know how you feel

And because you are sons, God has sent the Spirit of His Son into our hearts, crying, "ABBA! FATHER!" Gal. 4:6-7.[1]

---

[1] *Outreach.*

OUR DAILY ALLOWANCE

I watched as his daddy handed him the dollar bill. His baby blue eyes got big and a grin spread quickly across his chubby little face. He danced about, waving it over his four-year-old head like banner. Nearly taking a tumble, he stumbled, righted himself, and then skipped into the living room to show his mommy.

"Look what I got!" He sang. "Looky, looky!" His mommy looked at his happy little face and asked,

"Did your daddy give that to you? Is that your allowance?"

"Yep... but what's allow'nce?" He asked his smile fading.

"Well, it's something that is given to you, kind of like a little present, to do with as you wish. Lots of children get an allowance. It teaches them how to spend their money wisely."

"Will I get some more allow'nce" he asked hopefully.

"Yes, when we can we will give it to you." That thought and the image of the ice cream cone he could buy later, made the little boy smile again.

We are all God's children. We too are given a allowance each day and that allowance is life itself. We don't know how great or how small God's allowance will be or how long we will receive it. These are things that only God knows. Teach me Lord to use my allowance of life wisely, perhaps even to give it away.

This is the day that the Lord hath made [It is my day], and I will rejoice and be glad in it.

Teach us to count our days that we may gain a wise heart. Psalm 90:12,[2]

---

[2] Unpublished

INDEBTEDNESS

We tried each payday to give the children an allowance. Sometimes there wasn't enough money to give an allowance and they had to wait till next time. But when they were fortunate enough, they received a dollar or two apiece. This was not for doing any chores because chores were something they were expected to do, but because we hoped they would learn to budget their money.

We had imagined them growing mature enough to save for something big they might like to have or at the very least, learning to spend it wisely. The older they got, the more allowance they were given, presumably because the older they were the more we expected them to handle their money wisely. I'm not sure how successful our plan was, but in retrospect, I would still give them an allowance, though I might insist they save a portion of it rather than hope they would save it. Ah well, like they say, hindsight is 20/20.

As with all children, it was not uncommon for them to feel that money burning a hole in whichever pocket it was in. Sometimes itchy fingers would spend that money on the first thing that caught their eye.

How many times did I roll my eyes when they bought a hamburger? "You have food at home," I would say.

"But not like this," they would retort.

Sometimes they would spend half of their allowance on those 25 cent bobble machines, hoping to get a cheap little ring that would be forgotten or broken by the time we got home.

There were times when they lost their allowance before we ever got out of the house. It seemed they had a little less respect for their allowance since it was a gift and not something they had earned. There were even times when they would wisely save their money until the next payday, but most of the time I was left wondering "what we were doing wrong?" I hated to interfere; after all, it was their money. I gave it to them to spend.

There was one thing they often did that always astounded me. Sometimes they would give their allowance to a sibling who just had to have this or that. Sometimes the money would be repaid and sometimes not. Sadly, I had to watch the indebted sibling struggle through that glorious moment of receiving an allowance only to have to give it up to pay a debt. Sometime the loan-giver forgave the debt. This allowance giving ritual continued until the children started working and earned spending money.[3]

---

[3] *Outreach*

AMAZING

The history of man is amazing. Beginning with the disobedience of Adam and Eve, and immediately continuing with Cain and Abel, our history is an accumulation of one horrendous crime after another. For centuries man has participated in a multitude of crimes against God, man and creation. Oh, there is an occasional random of act of kindness, a monumental display of courage, even a martyr every now and then, but as marvelous as these may be, they can hardly balance the scales.

The scripture is a reflection of mankind. The Old Testament is a smorgasbord of cowards, scoundrels and disobedient children. It is long awaited and short lived obedience peppered with Godly admonitions and promises resulting in the need for continual forgiveness.

The New Testament is the same food with a different name; only in the New Testament we meet the great IAM, Jesus, face to face. Jesus does the unthinkable. He loves the unlovable. He approaches the unapproachable. He touches the untouchable. He mixes His Love with His blood and offers it to whomsoever. Like a spiritual flood, He washes away the old to make way for the new.

Scripture reflects not just man collectively, but individually. My name is written between the lines. I am the subject, understood. I am saint and sinner. I am Judas and John. I am lost and I am found. I am blind, yet I can see. I am not worthy, yet, I am saved. We are not worthy of His attention much less His love, yet He died for us. Yes he died to cover it all up, to bury it, to end it. Why does He do this?

It is easier for me to understand that we are worthless and undesirable, but, a limitless love? How could He? Why would He? Why should He? I don't know why, but praise God He does it in spite of me. He does it in spite of us. He does it in spite of all we have done. He does it because of His love and His.... Amazing grace....

How sweet the sound, that saved a wretch like me.
I once was lost, but now...I'm found.
I was blind oh, but now I see.
'Twas grace that taught my heart to fear,
and grace my fear relieved.
How precious did that grace appear?
The hour I first believed.

For the grace of God that brings salvation, appeared to all men. It teaches us to say "no" to ungodliness and worldly passions and to live self-controlled, upright and godly lives in this present age, while we wait for The blessed hope, the glorious appearing of our great God and Savior, Jesus Christ, who gave Himself for us to redeem us from all wickedness and to purify for Himself a people that are His very own, eager to do what is good.

Titus 2:11-14 NIV[4]

---

[4] *Outreach*

LET'S PLAY

He stands motionless, his body wet with perspiration. The night air is thick and his face and arms glisten from the humidity. The sinews in his neck stand at attention and the muscles in his cheek throb rhythmically. Large droplets of sweat roll down his face, leaving a muddy trail through the dust that covers him from head to foot.

From a distance, it is hard to perceive the slight nod of his head and the flare of his nostrils. Though his eye lids rest half closed, staring vacantly straight ahead, he is keenly alert. He senses without turning, the offensive opponent to the left and to the right of him. Like a hawk, he studies this newest opponent standing directly before him. His body tenses. His jaw slackens, and like a shot, he delivers with deadly force, that which his opponent has impatiently waited. The ball whizzes by and whoosh! Like a sword, the bat slices the tense air, instantly followed by a "STEE-RIKE!" The sound of judgment reverberates through the hot, night air to be followed by a crescendo of earthly admiration and applause.

In disappointment, the opponent turns away. He removes his helmet, only to swipe back his hair and replace it. The tension of the moment makes his hands damp. Resting the bat against his knee, he crouches down to grab a hand full of dirt. Rubbing the dirt between his hands he studies the pitcher. He is determined. A hush settles around him. Straightening himself, he taps the dirt from his cleats and returns to the plate. Mumbling something under his breath, he takes his stance, stirring the air with his bat. His grip is so firm his knuckles turn white and the freckles on his hands nearly shine. Knees bent, eyes glued to the mound, and barely breathing, he waits again to test his skill against the goliath before him.

I wish that life were a game, but it is not. I wish that sin and evil did not exist, but they do. I wish that Jesus didn't have to die on the cross, but so glad He did. I wish that it was easy to fight an unseen enemy, but it most certainly is not.

Lord, help me to return to the war even if I lose a battle. Teach me to recognize my mortal enemy and to love my brother. Remind me Lord that you are my strength and to realize that I am never alone. And when I it is time for me to leave this life, I pray that I can say,
"I have fought the good fight, I have finished the race, and I have kept the faith."[5]

---

[5] *Outreach*

BORN YESTERDAY?

I have no name,

I have no home.

I have no parents,

Nor do I have any love.

I have no beautifully decorative nursery,

And I don't have any dolls or colorful toys.

I have no past, present, or future to share;

I have no hopes of ever reaching the stars.

I'll never be able to show the world what I can be,

And I'll never have the chance to grow old and wise.

Why, you ask?

Because, I wasn't born yesterday,

But I was supposed to be.

Kari Gunter

THE CHURCH

Recently, I took another lap around the wilderness. My ego trip began after I tripped over a rather large stumbling stone. I regained my balance in time to discover that I had fallen over my own feet and taken a lonely tumble. Falling down should make you pay more attention to where you are going and where you are stepping. In my profound reasoning, I had stepped out of the church, but all things work together for good to those who love the Lord and are called...*according to His purpose*. And we are called to be His Church; His beloved Bride.

I am learning about the Church. Not my church or your church, but His Church. I have learned that I do indeed see in the looking glass dimly. I see only shadows, because I look with the eyes of my limited mind sometimes seeing only what I want to see. The Jews looked at Jesus and didn't see the Messiah and their spiritual salvation, because they wanted to see something and someone else, but through the eyes of faith, the shadows become clearer, and I do not always like what I see. I see me, primping in front of the mirror, trying to make myself look good, sacrificing His Purpose for my ideas. I have seen not only the things that are, but see the connection to the things that were and are to be. I have seen His Church, nameless, faceless and ageless. I see it racing through time in a relay race that is nearing the finish line carrying the baton, His Word, handing it from generation to generation...not from one denomination to another...but from one believer to another...from you to me...to...the next child of God.[6]

---

[6] *The Mustard Seed*

GOLDIE

The TV alarm goes off. It's 5:45 am. I groan. Fifteen minutes later, I'm still *thinking* about getting out of the bed. Finally, I make a half-hearted effort by opening my eyes. I stretch, but get caught short when a muscle in my back cramps. Augh!! I try to relax, but it's no use, I've got to get up.

Groping for my glasses, I roll out of the bed. I put on my slippers and bathrobe. Stiffly I shuffle down the hall and into the kitchen, leaving my husband to watch the morning news through half-opened eyes. Like a robot, I put on the go juice; coffee. A few minutes later, with two cups in hand, I shuffle back toward the bedroom. I give my husband his coffee then head toward the bathroom to begin my morning rituals.

I shower, dry my hair, brush my teeth and put on my oil of Olay. After dressing, I walk briskly back to the kitchen. Now my husband can begin his morning routines.

Feeling like a new woman, I grab another cup of coffee and a bite to eat. I make our lunches and sometimes I even remember to put something out for supper. At 7:15, with a jug of water in hand, I head out the door to find Goldie waiting, shivering in the morning frost.

I awaken her with a turn of the key. She is cranky. I let her idle for a while to warm up. I slosh a little water on her frosted windshield and start the wipers-a few minutes later, I'm heading up and out the driveway. We move slowly at first, until she catches her breath. The coughing and sputtering stops by the time we get to the Sandersville Highway. Goldie is warmed up now and going good.

I hate to report that Goldie and I have a lot in common. We weren't bad looking when we were young, but now we both move a lot slower since our *get up and go got up and went*. I wear a layer of cover girl and Goldie wears a coating of kaolin; it's obvious, we both could use a good make over. The reason we have a lot in common is that we're both getting old.

Goldie is only 16 years old, but in car years she is well beyond middle aged, so that makes her older than me, though there is an obvious similarity between my uphill disabilities and hers. Let's see...if a dog ages 7 years for every human one, then a car must age about 6 for every human year. If the average life expectancy for an automobile is 10-12 years, then she is well over the hill at 96 that means she's in better shape for her age than I am for mine! Hmm, I don't think I like where this is going...

Speaking of going...driving the same route to work every day for six years has caused me to meet some of the same people on the highway, over and over again. More precisely, I have met some of the same cars on the highway causing us to lose our human personalities and take on automotive ones. In fact, I wouldn't recognize the drivers if they bit me. For instance, there's this impudent little red Civic that scoots past us every day and an arrogant gray Dodge Ram that roars past, leaving us eating dirt. Those young whippersnappers! I want you to know that occasionally, I do get the thrill of passing an RV, if it happens to be going uphill. Then there are those massive, egotistical kaolin trucks.

I cannot count on my fingers and toes the times I have been run off the road or forced to pull over by a crass and cocky, red-green-orange kaolin truck in a fever to get wherever it was going. It's not just the issue of highway etiquette: it reeks of a major disrespect for life. I don't know how much they earn on kaolin run, but I do know that my life is worth more than those few bucks. Are they trying to commit vehicular homicide?

Approaching the four lanes of the James C. Carr Highway, a whole string of cars impatiently passes by. What's the hurry, anyway? We'll be rearranged, but we'll all meet at the same traffic light downtown in just a few minutes.[7]

---

[7] *Union Recorder*

THE MIRACLE

It was still dark when I pulled out of the drive way on a cold, Monday morning. The depth of darkness was a little unusual, but I guessed it was because of the clouds. The rain that had plagued us for days was stubbornly clinging to the sky. I didn't pay much attention to the darkness as I drove to work, but traveling due east it is difficult to ignore certain things like the sunrise!

I could barely see the outline of the dark clouds hanging in the sky until the first stream of sunlight shot into the darkness followed by another, and yet another. In the blinking of an eye, the sun revealed a rippling ocean of black clouds straining to escape the horizon. As the sun crept heavenward those black clouds melted into crimson. The change was spectacular. As far as the eye could see, the entire expanse was blood red.

The sun continued its journey. Within minutes, crimson faded into pink and finally the clouds became a frothy white. Beyond, the pale blue sky deepened to a vivid blue. And soon those treacherous clouds were nothing more than dissipating vapors. It left me praising God.

Some people may find a demon behind every bush, but sometimes I can see God everywhere. I don't think this to be some wondrous gift that God has bestowed on me, but rather merely the result of just knowing who he is. For those who know him, it is not difficult to see his handiwork all around, for to see his creation, is to see Him. If I had merely witnessed the miracle of an awakening day, I would be blessed, but if I revisited the miracle of my salvation, I am once again, eternally blessed.

Romans 1:20-21a ever since God created the world, His invisible qualities, both His eternal power and His divine nature, has been clearly seen; they are perceived in the things that God has made. So those people have no excuse at all! They know God but they do not give Him the honor that belongs to Him, nor do they thank Him. (TEV)[8]

---

[8] Unpublished

DEATH OR LIFE?

They say there are two things we can be sure of doing in this life and that is to pay taxes and die. There is one more thing the majority of us want to know, what happens after we die?

Most people have come to realize that yes; we will continue to exist after this body dies. Birth is the just the beginning of our great adventure into eternity. Why some pass through this life sooner than others, remains a mystery. Though it is evident that death will arrive, some of us are prepared for the trip and some are not. In fear and trembling some of us wait, dreading the unknown, while some of us wait in excited anticipation for what we have seen with our hearts.

These are the earthly facts; once we are born we will die, taxes or no taxes. The answer to the big question seems beyond our understanding, yet it is within our grasp ... we control where we will spend eternity.

`We had a death in our family recently. My husband's Uncle Robert passed silently away leaving us behind to continue our journey without him. I suppose as lives go, and to the casual observer, Uncle Robert lead an uneventful life. He never married and had no children. He spent the last 23 years in a nursing home and the past several years he lived mostly confined. He lost daily contact with his family, friends and his church. He had the occasional visitor, but for the most part, life was passing him by, or rather, he was passing slowly through life, closing in on that monumental, earth-shattering moment that is the end of the beginning and the beginning of forever. He teetered on the temporal then slipped quietly into the eternal. Uncle Robert was prepared. He left his emotional baggage behind and rode into eternity wearing only his faith.

There are times I feel that life is like a train ride, speeding through time. I am not the engineer, but the passenger. I didn't ask to ride; I just woke up one day and found myself speeding along life's highway. Sometimes I just watch as life speeds by and sometimes I investigate whenever we stop to rest. Always the train keeps moving onward to the next stop and places unknown. Where will I disembark? Who will be left to continue the trip with me? Are we late or are we early? Only the conductor knows.[9]

---

[9] Unpublished

IT'S ALMOST SUPPERTIME

Mema and PaPa lived in a big, white frame house on the corner of Forest and Cypress streets. In Valdosta Georgia the summers get mighty hot. Theirs was an older neighborhood old houses, old folks. The street had been widened several times over the years so that the edge of the road was now less than 15 feet to the porch. There were no curbs or sidewalks, just the big old camphor tree, the dirt and roadway.

On one particular day years ago, my husband and I and our six children, were visiting Valdosta for the week. The weather was typically hot and muggy. It was almost lunch time. The air was still without the slightest hint of a breeze. The children had been playing in the back yard and now were being herded into the house to wash up for lunch.

It is not a quiet event, rounding up six children under the age of 12. Amidst all the commotion I didn't miss our three-year-old. She was here just a moment ago. She didn't answer when I called her name. I looked in all the rooms. I found nothing. I walked to the front porch and pushed open the wooden screen to look out. My heart stopped.

There she was happily playing in the dirt beside the road. Not six inches away, cars pulled up to stop before making a right turn. She didn't see me and I was afraid to call her name because of all the what-ifs rattling around inside my head. Sliding quietly out the door, I walked behind her and scooped her up, startling her. She cried, as I carried her to the porch. She wanted to play in the dirt. My heart pounded when I saw how close the cars were coming to her.

She complained all the way to the bathroom. She was hot and sticky and covered from head to foot is black soot-like dirt. I intended to just wash her hands and face so she could eat, but she was such a mess. There was no way around it. She had to be bathed.

I quickly ran water into the four-footed tub and stripped her down to her birthday suit. Lifting her over the side I placed her in the tub and began scrubbing. In no time she was shiny as a copper penny. She smelled so good and was so kissable. I put clean clothes on her and combed her wispy hair, chatting with her and calling her by her nick name, Tatty. Picking her up, I carried her into the dining room, placed her in her own little highchair and pushed her to the table. I cut up her food for her and placed it on a cute little plate. She ate her fill and afterward she lay down with me on the big bed. She stretched out beside me, limbs akimbo, oblivious to the world around her. Without a care in the world she fell into a peaceful sleep.

Oh, Abba. Thank you for rescuing me from this world. Thank you for cleansing me and clothing me in your righteousness. Thank you for being there for me when I needed you speaking to me as only you can. Thank you for caring for me and for supplying all my needs. Thank you for making me feel safe and secure. Thank you for giving me your peace. Thank you for saving me.[10]

---

[10] Unpublished

SEEKING WHOM HE MAY DEVOUR

I had just come in from work. My mother-in-law and the two youngest girls were home as well when the phone rang. On the other end, my brother's wife, Jeanette, said the words no parent ever wants to hear.

There was an accident. Injuries. Hospital, but, Becky, is Becky all right? "Is she alive?" I ask hesitantly.

We can deal with anything, if she is alive. A moment's hesitation, "she was when they took her in the ambulance." Time stands still as those words burn their way into my brain.

My mother-in-law watches me, knowing something is wrong. Hanging up the phone my heart leaps to my lips, "Oh, Jesus, she's just a baby...!" Who said that? I don't even recognize that it is my voice that is crying out.

My heart is racing. I pace the room. I've got to get to the hospital. She's only 11, Lord. I'm shaking. My husband, where is he? Out of town, remember? I've got to get to the hospital. The boys, where are the boys? They've gone camping. I'm in no condition to drive. I call Sylvia and she says, "Let's go." I'm out on the driveway before she can crank the car. I promise everyone I'll call as soon as I can. I'm scared. I'm shivering. My mind is cold and blank, but in my heart I pray, "Please God, don't let her die"

By the time we make it to the emergency room, my husband is already there. How did he know? I don't think to ask out loud. My mom, my brother and his family and friends are arriving. The doctors won't let us see her. I'm scared. I'm not sure if I can stand to see her.

"What happened?" I hear someone ask. My eyes follow the conversation, I can't seem to talk.

"I didn't see the other car." I hear the pain and see the guilt in Jeanette's face. "I'm sorry..." it *was an accident.*

It wasn't that bad. The other driver had a broken foot. Everyone got out ok, but Becky wasn't breathing. Someone stopped. Cut her out of the seatbelt. CPR. Unconscious. He saved her! Who is he?

The doctors call us. We can see her now. Sending her to a bigger hospital 35 miles away. Brain trauma.

Kidney damage. They roll her past. She looks perfect. No blood, No scratches, just a life support system and tubes. Go. Follow behind. Oh, Jesus help us.

Sylvia drives. Husband in the front, and I'm in the back wrapped in a blanket. Rain. Lots of rain. Black asphalt wet and shiny, reflecting the car lights. We follow the turning red light. *Please keep her safe don't let her die out here.*

I am yet speechless. I pray, mumbling under my breath. I stop watching the ambulance ahead of us. I shut my eyes. I see her crumpled form with demons like flies hovering over her. I'm angry. "Get away, you can't have her! You can't have her!" I hear myself say aloud. They hear me too. I don't care. I shiver.

Another hospital. My spirit groans. More doctors. More machines. More tests. More waiting. More prayers. Three hours later, we finally get to see her. Her little body resting quietly aided by a breathing machine. More waiting. The chair is hard next to her bed. The TV is on to stimulate her. Questions. No answers. Tired. Waiting. Dawn. The first day...

Becky lived. A stranger passing the accident felt a strong urge to turn around and go back to the accident. He was an EMT, retired. When the ambulance arrived, they checked. She was unconscious, but breathing. When no one was looking, her breathing stopped. He brought her back. An angel in blue jeans. No lasting brain damage. No kidney damage. I praise God for answered prayer, and for strangers who are angels unaware.

I praise God that he allowed me to glimpse into the spiritual realm. I never doubted the existence of spiritual warfare, but now I have seen it. I experienced it. I fought it with prayer and He came through. The battle was won. One battle with so many more raging.

For we are not contending against flesh and blood, but against the principalities, against the powers, against the world rulers of this present darkness, against the spiritual hosts in heavenly places. Ephesians 6:12 RV[11]

---

[11] Unpublished

THE GLOVED HAND

I am late. Yanking open the car door, I pop the key into the ignition and give it a turn. The engine groans, coughs in the cold morning air, then takes off with a roar. I flick the switch for a quick swish of the windshield wipers, shift the defroster to high, then I throw it into reverse to back out of the driveway. The car sputters momentarily, but recovers. We're off.

A few minutes down the road, the car is warming up, but my hands are very cold. My gloves are in my purse sitting beside me. So, while keeping my eyes on the road, I grope inside my purse with my cold, right hand, quickly finding the first glove. I manage to put it on while flying down the highway.

Now, for the second glove. Reaching again into my purse, I fish again, but this time the seeking hand is gloved. I search, but I cannot feel the second glove. Frustrated, but still keeping my eyes on the road, I grab the purse and shake it a bit hoping to rearrange things and start the blind search again. I know it's there, but I cannot feel the other glove! Finally, I surrender, remove the glove from my right and reach into my purse with the naked hand. How easy it is to feel the second glove and retrieve it.

It astonishes me the things the Lord uses to teach His lessons. I could not find the glove because I could not feel it. How many times have I reached for heaven with a heart that is unable to feel His presence because it is wrapped up with other things? How many times have I tried to pray out of obligation and missed the groaning of the spirit within? How many times have I reached out to help, my eyes glued to the earth and only able to offer a gloved hand? How many times? Thank God the hand He offers is not covered with good intentions or obligation, but with His holy and precious blood. How glad I am to say "He touched me." He did not hide or pull away when He saw my spiritual leprosy; the sin that separates me from Him.

Mark chapter 6:

12. And it happened when he was in a certain city, that behold a man who was full of leprosy saw Jesus and he fell on his face and implored Him, saying, "Lord if You are willing, You can make me clean!"

13. Then He [Jesus] put out His hand and touched him, saying "I AM WILLING, BE CLEANSED." Immediately the leprosy left him. Just like the leper, He touched me, praise God, He touched me![12]

---

[12] *The Mustard Seed*

GREETINGS

From me to you
I send this greeting,
Only because it's easier
Than squeezing
An arm or a leg or
Parts not pleasing
Into an envelope
Too small for sending
All the prayers
That I've been praying
That God will bless
You, oh, so greatly.
I know when
The Lord was seeking
A few good men
His word for keeping,
He found you
Wide awake, not sleeping.
And neither rests He,
For He is busy keeping

An age-old promise

To hearts now aching.

"I am with you always."

So, keep on praying

For His Spirit

And keep on listening

And in His Word

Keep on believing.

Amen[13]

---

[13] Unpublished

HANDS

With his tiny hand the infant clasps my finger
And hangs on tightly.
My husband reaches absentmindedly for my hand
And brings it to his lips.
My child reaches up for my hand
And the guidance it offers.
My friend holds my hand
And prays for me.
I surrender my heart and reach for
Your Nail-scarred Hand
And hold on for dear life.
So that I too
Can reach out to help a friend[14]

---

[14] Unpublished

NO DAUGHTER OF MINE

She brushed her long dark hair away. A tear escapes, rolling down her cheek. Her ears were still ringing, "No daughter of mine would do that!" Even though she was outside in the yard those words came crashing through the walls of wood to break her heart.

The daddy was right you know. She shouldn't have lied. It was such a big lie too. Why did she allow herself to be sucked into such deceit? It sure didn't take long for her to realize she was in over her 11 year-old head. She just wasn't smart enough to think it through. She wasn't prepared for the growing snowball of lies that inevitably follow the first. She waited in fear; fear of no longer being loved. *Selah.*

Sliding behind the steering wheel, the mother slams the car door and stretched the seat belt across to the buckle. That's when she spotted a letter on the dash board, folded in half with "Mom and Dad" scribbled across the top. She froze. In that moment, she knew it was true. Their daughter had run away. Sitting in the dark she pondered the possible reasons."

No child of mine would run away," she argued. The hand-written letter answered some of her questions. The foster child, liberal and gay, influenced the daughter until she didn't know who she was. At 17, the daughter was fighting for her own identity and her own beliefs. Helping a child in need had nearly cost these parents their own daughter. *Selah.*

"No daughter of mine..." those faded words had wounded me like a knife. It took decades for me to recover. Oh, dad forgave me, but the experience left a scar. I knew I could never be good enough. History repeated itself when I heard those same judgmental words escape my own lips. Like a slap in the face, I was shocked into reality; the reality of spiritual warfare. In her confusion, our daughter thought we could not love her. So she left. We cried, we waited, we prayed. How great is the pain of a parent hurting for a child; how magnified must be God's anguish as He waits, yearning for His wayward children. Our daughter came home. Have you?

For I am certain that nothing can separate us from His love; neither death nor life, neither powers, neither the present nor the future, neither the world above nor the world below - there is nothing in all creation that will ever be able to separate us from the love of God which is ours through Christ Jesus our lord. Romans 8:38-39[15]

---

[15] *Outreach*

WHEN I GO

To my children:

   I wish I could leave you a fine inheritance; money, land or possessions. I wish I could, but I cannot. I wish I could leave behind my successes, like sunshine in which to bask. But I have none to leave. I wish I could leave you my courage, but I have little since I am a coward at heart. I wish I could leave my determination, but each of you in your special way taught me about true grit.

   I wish I could leave you faith, but even that is not mine to give, it is His gift to give to those who would seek it. I can leave you the knowledge that I love you, but I believe you know how much I love you. God knows that my husband and my family were my life and my love, but in failing Him I have failed myself and then you, **if** I have not left you with the knowledge of Who loves you the most.

   I'm sorry I was not the Christian example I should have been in each of my earthly roles. I'm sorry if you grieve when I am gone. I never meant to hurt you. I'm sorry I grieved the Spirit with my procrastination. I'm sorry I did not tell you about His Love over and over again. I am just so sorry I did not believe Him for **all** things.

   So then, I guess I really have nothing to leave you except these words: Jesus loves you. He loved me. He is mine because He chose me. I did not earn His love, and I certainly did not deserve it. Even if I had really, really tried, I could not have done enough in this life to thank Him for that love. It was mine only by grace.

I regret I will leave you with apologies and beg your forgiveness. I will miss you for awhile, but we will meet again and embrace. Be of good cheer...it is indeed well with my soul. Oh, how I look forward to the moment when I shall see Him as he really is, to hear His voice and to sing His praise. I want that so much, *to sing to Him* forever; as one voice in a joyful multitude. Oh, our God **is** an Awesome God! With tears of joy I will sing His praise and anxiously await the day when each of you will stand beside me and we can sing His Song together.[16]

---

[16] Unpublished

I SAW A SERMON TODAY

Today, while going about the everyday chore of living, I saw a sermon. Matter of fact, I saw more than one sermon today. I wasn't in church, the choir wasn't singing, and amen's did not echo from the rafters. I didn't hear a single word, but nevertheless, I saw a sermon today.

It was a quiet sermon, spoken with actions rather than with words. It took place today when I saw a man graciously hold the post office door open for a lady burdened with packages.

I witnessed it when an out-of-town visitor offered an old man a glass of water in the nursing home.

My heart was moved by the youngster who led the sobbing toddler back to his lost mother.

My heart was pricked at the generosity of a good Samaritan helping a stranded motorist jump start his car.

Gazing into the mirror, I argue, "But anyone can be nice! Even non-Christians!

To be nice by nature or to be obedient by choice, are two different things. To sacrifice self leaves room for the love of God, *my heart beats back*.

Well, that woman in the post office, I know her. She is not a Christian; she's not even nice." I counter.

Jesus died for her.

"And that poor little boy, his mother is a drug user"

Jesus bled for them both.

"And the old man at the nursing home, he's out of his mind, he doesn't even know his own name!"

Jesus weeps for His children...

"And that motorist, he is a drunk!"

Before He could respond, I knew, but for the grace of God, go I.

Jesus said if you have done it unto the least of these my brethren, you have done it unto me.

"What have I done today for you Jesus," I question the mirror? Silence is the answer.

So, more than a living sermon am I like the little teapot, spouting a lot of steam, then sitting and waiting for God to reach down, tip me over to pour ME out?

Me, me, me. My daily sermons are all about me. It is written, "Do unto others as you would have them do unto you."

But the world erroneously repeats "Do unto others BEFORE they do it to you!"

A kind action will be remembered long after the most religious words can be recalled. If you do not love your brother, the love of God is not in you.

Forgive me.

Yes, I saw a sermon today. I saw it, but I didn't speak it, worse yet, I didn't live it. Today someone saw only **me** and not *Jesus in me*. I now see that the world is like a starving man and only after he is fed will I have his attention. I pray that beginning today, I am a living sermon and that this sermon consists of but a single word....Jesus.[17]

---

[17] *The Mustard Seed*

I SEARCHED FOR GOD

I knew
That God was real
But I couldn't find him.

I asked
A holy man and he said
Seek and you will find.

I looked
To the heavens and saw
Only the stars.

I questioned
Philosophies and returned
With contradictions.

I entertained
The spirits and felt
Only fear.

I studied
Books on mathematics
And came back confounded.

I listened
To political debates
And returned angry.

I witnessed
Man's cruelty
And felt hopelessness.

I observed
The power of nature
And I felt helpless.

Then I
I read the Bible
And I found
The cross.

Looking up
I saw Jesus
And found
My God.[18]

---

[18] Unpublished

WHEN IT HURTS

I stand at the sink absent-mindedly washing dishes and looking out the window. I see his reflection as he walks up behind me. He is taller than me now; a child in a man's body. His body language reveals volumes. I sense the pain and rejection in his young heart.

"Are you ok son?" I ask without turning, steadily washing dish after dish.

I watch his reflection. An eternity passes. Then, silently, he lowers his head, resting his chin on my shoulder. My hands stop their busy-ness. I feel his tears falling onto my blouse burning a hole in my heart.

"I didn't know it would hurt so much..." is all he can whisper.

Turning I take my 16 year-old son in my arms and let him cry. With each sob my heart aches. Growing up is so hard.

"I know." I offer through my own sob.

"It'll be all right," I promise him, trying to convince myself. In resignation, I sigh

"Sometimes, it hurts to love."

"I asked Jesus, "How much do you love me?'
"This much.' He replied. Then he stretched out his hands and died on the cross." *(Anon)*

FOR GOD SO LOVED THE WORLD THAT HE GAVE..."

Yes, sometimes it hurts to love.[19]

---

[19] Unpublished

UPC AND THE CROSS

I love a bargain. I love to buy on sale and think I pulled a slick one over the retailer. I'm so silly. If, it's too good to be true" it probably is. I can only think of one spiritual exception to this natural law, otherwise, that old saying, "nothing is free" is a wise observation.

There is a price tag on everything, except perhaps, that box of cereal on the grocer's shelf that I want to buy. There's no longer a price tag on the cereal box because now there is the UPC symbol. UPC, UNIVERSAL PRODUCT CODE, computer coding, that allows the retailer to systematically price, monitor, and replenish his merchandise at any given time. Great for him, bad for me. UPC labeling is supposed to have sub-titles on the shelf, translating this computer lingo so you and I can tell how much each item costs. How many times have I gotten to the checkout to discover the UPC symbol pricing was incorrect or even non-existent? How many times have I been misled about the cost only to discover the price is higher than I thought? At this point, it becomes a choice. If I want the item, I pay the price. If I have second thoughts, I have to decide if it is worth the cost.

The one spiritual exception I spoke of is the cost of salvation. To us who believe, salvation is free, but it had its price and it was not cheap. As a matter of fact, it was so expensive, no one except Jesus could pay the price and the cost to Him, was the cross. UPC, ULTIMATE PERSONAL COST. Jesus knew the cost and was willing to pay that price. So now, I am debt free, yet I am indebted to the One who paid it all.

For you are bought with a price; therefore glorify God in your body and your spirit, which are God's. Matthew 6:20 NKJ[20]

---

[20] *Outreach*

TRASH OR TREASURE

My husband mutters under his breath as he gathers up the trash from the four corners of the house. Recycling is serious business with him and he just found some cans in with the trash. Woe is me. He ignores the odor and reaches past the unmentionable trash and retrieves the cans. Augh!! All that for a couple of cans! Now that's dedication! Even though it is a nuisance, I believe in my heart that recycling must be done. And I DIDN'T PUT THAT CAN IN WITH THE TRASH! I know that's what he's thinking. As he drags each bag to his truck to take to the recycling center, I do my part by putting a new trash bag back into the trash can. Whew.

I like these trash bags. I buy them you know, when I do the shopping. They aren't the usual dark green or black poly-whatever trash bags, they are clear. I like clear. Clear is the reason my husband knew a foreign object was in with the trash. He could see it. As I put the box of trash bags back into the utility closet, it occurs to me that we are like trash bags.

We spend a lifetime of accumulating stuff. Oh, not just in the garage or the attic, but inside us. We become a hodge-podge of stuff like vices, virtues, habits, traits, likes and dislikes, prejudices, secret desires, and sins. All this is buried deep inside us; the trash mixed in with the treasure. The problem is we think we are like the dark green trash bags and that no one can see what's on the inside. But sometimes the unseen rubbish inside punctures or penetrates the trash bag and pretty soon the whole mess comes tumbling out. Yuck.

I'm beginning to realize that we are like a clear trash bag and only God can see what's truly on the inside. And only God cares enough to dig deep down into that stinky, smelly trash to remove what is not desirable, cast it away and recycle what is left.

Lord, I thank you that you are willing to take this mess and make a masterpiece.

Create in me a clean heart oh, God,

And renew a right spirit within me.

Caste me not away from thy presence,

And take not thy Holy Spirit from me.

Restore unto me the joy of thy Salvation

And uphold me with thy free spirit. Psalm 51:10[21]

---

[21] *Outreach*

A VIEW FROM THE BACK OF THE ROOM

Entering at the front of the classroom near the blackboard, the new girl walks cautiously into the classroom. Hugging her tattered notebook tightly to her chest, she extends the transfer papers to the teacher with her free hand. Eons pass as she awaits the verdict.

"Hello Sarah. There is a desk there in the last row that you can take. It's nice to have you in our class. My name is Ms. Adams."

The last row! That's great! She mumbles her thanks to the teacher and glances up just long enough to locate the empty seat. With her eyes cast downward she makes a bee-line for the empty seat, walking through rows of school desks standing in military formation. She marches past each desk with her eyes seeing only tennis shoes. She sees black ones, white ones, multi-colored ones, short and tall ones. Gratefully she doesn't see the faces that own them. She couldn't bear that just yet. It's bad enough she can feel their stares. That short trip takes forever, but she finally reaches her destination. She glides her plump, teen form into the one-size-fits-all plastic desk. Ah, it fits. Her first concern is out of the way.

By the time she parks her purse and notebook under her seat the teacher places an English quiz in front of her saying,

"Give it a try, Sarah."

Returning to the blackboard, the repeats "You have 15 minutes to complete this quiz. Begin now."

Resting her cheek in the palm of her left hand, Sarah leans forward to study the sheet. Her long dark hair cascades around her oval face, allowing her a short reprieve from the curious eyes that occasionally peek back at her. Sneaking a look through her long bangs, she studies the bobbing heads in front of her. They all look so unfriendly. What is it that waits for her? Who are these people? It's like this every time they have to move. New faces. Faces with long hair, short hair; black, brown, red and blonde hair. All different, but all the same, still strangers. They are all hunched over the page just like her. Her thoughts return to the quiz. It is easy. One by one the heads pop up, turning the page over to indicate completion.

Looking up, she pushes her hair behind her ear and turns her page over. There is a shoulder-length red head with pink tennis shoes, sitting directly in front. Pink tennis shoes, looks up as she turns the quiz over. Turning to reach under her desk for her notebook, she looks over her right shoulder, smiles, and then winks at Sarah. Hmm, maybe this place will be ok after all.

This is just to illustrate a thought. Perhaps we have each been there; the new kid on the block, the class room, the church, or the job. Sometimes I think one of the things that can defuse a potentially unhappy situation is something as small as a smile.[22]

---

[22] *Outreach*

WISH YOU WERE HERE!

She drops her pocket book onto the dining room table, rattling the salt and pepper shakers. Tossing today's bills on the table, she turns the shiny postcard over to look again at the beautiful rendition of heaven on the reverse side.

"We miss you. Wish you were here." It was signed by her Sunday school teacher.

"Yeah, I wish I were there too. It beats this dump," she grumbles, tossing the card carelessly onto the table. It bounces off the cereal bowl caked with this morning's dried up Rice Krispies. She strolls over to the refrigerator. It's been a long hard day. Tomorrow will be no better. But maybe tomorrow will at least feel better. This has been an eerie, dreary day.

"Wish you were here, indeed," she continues grumbling as she opens the refrigerator door. She stands gazing into the cool whiteness wondering what to have for supper. As usual, she forgot to put something out this morning. She's too tired to cook and decides to have scrambled eggs and toast; a perfect ending to a perfect day.

One behind the other, she turns on the 6:00 news and the gas under the frying pan. In a few minutes the eggs and toast are ready and the news commentator is talking about the Middle East.

"I'm a regular gourmet cook," she mumbles to no one, as she sets her plate on the table and returns to the kitchen for her cup of coffee. Back at the table, she sets her coffee down on the colorful postcard. Unexpectedly, the curtains stir at the window and a ray of sunshine escapes the cloudy sky to find its way into the tiny kitchen. The TV drones on in the background.

The eggs need salt and the salt shaker is empty. Groaning, she gets up to fetch the box of salt from the cabinet. She's tired. She's always tired. She's too tired to do much of anything, especially go to church. Returning to the table she discovers that the box of salt is empty as well. She slams the box down jiggling the shakers again.

"That's just great!" She moans, slumping down in the chair. She pushes the plate of now boring eggs away and munches unhappily on the dry toast. That's when she hears it. The steady sound starts out low and grows until it's nearly deafening. People outside are shouting and the sound of a fender-bender in progress carries up to her second story apartment. The TV suddenly goes black.

She picks up her cup of coffee and walks over to the window. Peaking out the window she sees some confusion over an auto accident. It doesn't look too serious so she turns away. A final breeze finds its way past her, lifting the postcard and twirling it around until it falls silently to the floor. That sound has stopped.

The sky begins to cloud up again. The TV is back on, but there's a different announcer in front of the camera this time and this one seems upset. She rushes over to turn up the volume picking the post card up off the floor and tossing it into the trash can. It falls up against the empty salt box with the "Wish you were here" side up, then slides down deeper into my daughter's trash can.

"Behold, I show you a mystery; we shall not all sleep, but we shall all be changed, in a moment, in the twinkling of an eye, at the last trump, for the trumpet shall sound and the dead shall be raised incorruptible and we shall be changed."

Hallelujah!

I just wish we'd all been ready...[23]

---

[23] *Outreach*

BEYOND

In silence he stood straight and tall
Through the questions and lies.
Struggling to stand they slapped him, whipped him,
And stripped him naked.
He would not raise one hand in his own defense.
He looked beyond.
He stumbled down the road on bloody feet
As they beat him with their obscenities and insults.
He fell in weariness; they picked him up.
He bled; they laughed. He didn't scream for justice.
He looked beyond.
His body rebelled as they dragged him
To his punishment and death.
He knew what was coming.
He didn't struggle or swear
As they finished their grisly job.
He looked beyond.
They raised him high and planted his cross
In the earth, tearing muscle from bone
And crushing the air from him.
Splinters dug into his bleeding back and his legs,
He convulsed as he gasped for air.
Yet, He looked beyond.
As they gambled for his garments as his blood soaked the
wood and fell to the earth below.

His body burned with pain, every fiber screaming
For release,
He looked beyond.
He saw all humanity huddled at the foot of his cross;
An endless, ageless procession of
The unloved and the unlovely;
The widowed, the aged, and the fatherless;
The cheaters, liars, and thieves;
The perverted, undisciplined, and self-righteous;
The ailing, forgotten and forlorn.
Tears of compassion mingled with tears of pain.
And he looked beyond.
The darkening sky hid the light.
The earth groaned and the rocks wept.
Thunder angrily rolled and the wind stood breathless;
All creation grew silent in fear.
Heaven was poised and ready as the angels strained
To heed his slightest command
And the demons cowered in the darkness.
Opening his eyes and looking below
he saw beyond those faces.
He looked beyond our guilt and beyond time.
Chest heaving, blood falling, strength ebbing,
He raised himself one last time and shouted,
"IT IS FINISHED!"
The sound of it still echoes in the earth.
What wondrous love is this that looks beyond Himself
To see our need?[24]

---

[24] *50's + Magazine*

ONE WAY TICKET

The flight from Heathrow to Atlanta is long and tiring. Vacations are not always a time of relaxation. I rest my head against the window, watching the world fly by. The DC-10 rises steadily through the smattering of clouds until we are engulfed in a silent, white world. The cloudy formations create a mystical world. The pristine whiteness takes my breath away.

Oblivious to the sudden turbulence, I marvel at the scene below. Do I recognize mountains and valleys? Do I see waves on an ocean of white, rising and falling upon shimmering sand? And in the brightness, is that my Lord calling to me?

I long to leave behind these wings of steel and the invisible chains of life. I yearn to fly into this silent white world that seems to whisper heaven's name. Wearily, I close my eyes. Instantly I find myself floating upward; into the whiteness and a bright world full of welcome and warmth. I revel in the pure ecstasy of freedom as I move upwards.

The hushed rumble of distant thunder causes me to gaze about this cloud land of joy. I see a soul streak past, and soon another! I see souls springing up everywhere breaking through the clouds like blades of wispy white grass. Together, we race toward heaven, following Him.

Our excitement mounts as we approach the light. Joy so fills my heart, that I think it might burst, but instead, my joy spills out of me as new song. Not only I, but as far as the eye can see, every soul flying upward is singing and praising God. Faster we fly. Upward we speed until we burst through the clouds and into the glorious light of heaven. We are followed by the sound of our music. The volume increases and the numbers increase. And the souls keep coming, singing and praising God, until the Place is filled from horizon to horizon; the sounds of praise become our very heartbeat. Joining the angels we complete the heavenly harmony. And every eye is focused on the Bright and Morning Star. Each note of our heart's song hangs suspended, like shimmering stars, reflecting His marvelous light. Our hearts belong to Him. With our hearts we adore Him; with our lips we bless and praise Him.

Then the music stops. Elohim looks up raising His right hand. The impact of His holiness causes some of us to faint. We can still hear the cherubim crying "Holy, Holy, Holy..." and I weep softly as He gently speaks, "Welcome Home, my good and faithful servants, welcome home."

30. Then the sign of the Son of Man will appear in heaven, and then all the tribes of the earth will mourn, and they will see the son of Man coming on the clouds of heaven with power and great glory.

31. And He will send Hi[25]s angels with a great sound of a trumpet and they will gather together His elect from the four winds, from one end of heaven to the other.

Matthew Chapter 24-17. Then we who are alive and remain shall be caught up together with them in the clouds to meet the Lord in the air. And thus we shall always be with the Lord.

18. Therefore, comfort one another with these words.

I Thessalonians Chapter 4

[25] Unpublished

WAKE UP

Scout is a pretty good old dog. He is very laid back. He rarely barks and he stays near the house pretty well. For a dog, he's a bit of a ham. He makes a great show of stalking and chasing our neighbor's cats, but I know those cats aren't the least bit afraid of him.

Because of past abuse, Scout no longer is able to wag his tail, so instead he flashes you a great big ear-to-ear grin. This ability makes him quite the conversation piece. Yep, Scout is a pretty good old dog.

Scout does, however, have one bad habit; he sleeps on the deck just outside the sliding door. The bad part is that he will not move from his resting place even when I attempt to step out the door. He just rolls over with his paws in the air, and grins at me.

"Move, Scout!" I say impatiently. He just lays there, his tongue lolling out, he remains motionless. Nudging him with my foot I repeat louder, "Move Scout!"

Nothing. It's as if he is dead.

If I want to get out the door, I have to take a giant step over his limp, little body. I have accepted this fact. So, if he's lying outside the door, I automatically step over him as if he doesn't exist and continue about my business.

I think a lot of us are like Scout. We see and hear things happening around us and, we just lie motionless in the same comfy spot. Who would we gripe to anyway? Who would care? So we just smolder and smoke to friends, family and any captive audience we run across. In essence, we have trained others to step over our apparently disinterested bodies while we just lie there grinning, not wanting to rock the boat.

But look closely. Inside this quiet, little dog rumbles a tumult of emotions. And how do I know? Now there is a Direct Line in the Union Recorder! And the sleeping dogs have found a reason to wake up.

Whether I agree or not, it is great to hear what others have to say and what they are thinking and feeling, I believe the direct line anonymity offers gives us the courage to say our piece, but at least we are speaking out and not lying quietly by in frustration.

Just between you and me, I do have one fear. One day, at a most unexpected time, sweet, quiet little Scout may just decide to jump up and ... OUCH![26]

---

[26] *Union Recorder*

JUST LIKE ME

They're out there, I can feel it. They're behind desks, at PTA meetings and in the grocery stores. They're in the churches and synagogues. They watch Monday night football and laugh at Jerry Seinfeld. They struggle with finances and with their children. They hurt, they bleed and they die. They are ordinary people, just like me.

I've been accused of being an idealist. Now if you had accused me of being a lazy idealist or an uninvolved idealist I might have to give some credence to the accusation. But the snub here is against idealism. If I put my faith into the Judeo-Christian standard that was the foundational outline for this country, is that wrong? To be an idealist doesn't mean I ignore reality, it means that reality has forced me to seek the strength I need to survive.

I believe one of the most crippling thoughts I can have is that I am the only one with these feelings. I learned a valuable lesson during the tense days following the Rodney King trials. Many of us were afraid of the repercussions that could follow the trial. It was during this time, I witnessed something that touched my very soul. It was dusk and I was driving south on Columbia street. Fear rumbled in my gut and I just wanted to be home. As I passed a church I saw him outside the locked building. He was kneeling on the hard concrete sidewalk, prostrate in prayer. Like many of us, this lone black man sought the only source of help that was bigger than you, me and the problems we face. In my heart I was with him on that cold, hard sidewalk.

The Promise Keepers are idealistic also. They base their ideals not on an intellectual "-ism" or an "-ology" but on Holy Scripture handed down for thousands of years. This guidance has never become outdated or old-fashioned. I don't want to argue about what is written in the Scripture. I didn't write it, I just believe it. (You can argue with the author though, if you care to.)

Yeah, I know. You've put me out there in right field somewhere, trying to ignore me, hoping I'll die from exposure or loneliness. But that's OK. I know something you don't know. I'm not alone out there. There are lots of us out there, more than you'd care to think about. They are people of all races, colors, and creeds. They are idealists just like me who see the true reality of things.

That true reality is this; that if we don't make some grass root changes, if we don't get our homes and our lives in order, if we don't stand up for what is right, nothing will change for the better. The reality is we'll all go down in this Titanic of human affliction. We'll go down without a government-approved life jacket and not a soul will be left to throw out a lifeline. Something needs to be done and we're the ones to do it; together that is, with God.[27]

---

[27] Unpublished

WHAT SO PROUDLY WE HAIL

This month we went to Washington D.C.; the "we" being my husband, my mom and I. I really wasn't looking forward to the trip because I hate to ride long distances, but once again, I was blessed in spite of myself. I didn't realize how much I needed this trip. Heaven knows a 12-hour drive is not exactly what I needed to be reminded of *who I am.*

Just exactly **who am I** anyway? I was raised in the 'burbs' of California, but I lived in Georgia for 26 years and that by choice. In my estimation that makes me a good ole Georgia girl by gum. I am not crazy about cities, but I will have to make an exception for DC; because it is so lovely. (At least the parts I saw.) It does have some not-so-good stuff too. It has lots of lights, lots of cars, lots of people, lots of concrete, and lots of history.

We saw the sights as best we could. Unfortunately, we only made a small dent in the Smithsonian. (Figuratively speaking, of course) We saw lots of monuments and memorials. The artistry and architecture are stunning. We saw the JFK Theater for the Performing Arts, The National Cathedral, Mt. Vernon, Arlington House, and Arlington National Cemetery. Everything was so educational. The tour guides told us the historical significance at each site then added trivial information as well, bringing a little spice and life to our forefathers whom now we only see in stone.

It was nice to hear the guides and even the taxi drivers talk about our capitol with such respect and admiration. Their respect and admiration for this country even rubbed off on me. And that is just what I needed. There is so much negative stuff in the news these days. Just turning on the TV is depressing. We're constantly bombarded with bad news like : how bad off everyone's economy is, how high taxes are, how low the educational scores are, how high the crime rate is, and how low down our president is. It's enough to give me a headache.

I want to tell you about some of my favorite sights in DC. The most impressive were the Iwo Jima, Vietnam, and Korean War Memorials. I was over whelmed at Iwo Jima and the Korean War monuments. It's hard to believe that the same creatures that make war can make something so emotionally moving.

Later, at the Vietnam War memorial, we found the name of a friend, and stood in silent respect with our memories. I hope he knows he's not forgotten. It was an emotional experience to look at the vast number of names on that wall.

Most were young just like we were when our friend died. Now I am old enough to be his mother. That is a sobering thought that makes my heart more sensitive to the cost of this national sacrifice. This time when I cried for the fallen, I cried as a mother cries for her children who are no more.

This cold black marble wall alone contains 58,217 children of America in the continuing cost of freedom and so many more can be added to that price tag. I am not always mindful of the cost of freedom, and memorials like these serve a worthwhile purpose, if only to remind me of the price we've paid for freedom.

You will be proud to know that our government is seeing to it that these wonderful monuments and memorials are kept clean and in good repair. Not only are there millions of Americans in DC every year, there are also many foreigners. Many of them are like me, seeing for the first time the Capitol city of America, the Land of the Free.

Yes, DC is a beautiful place, but you know, I can't help but wonder; when the **Do not disturb** sign is removed from the White House door, who will clean up the Presidency? Silly me. I don't have to think twice about that answer. I believe the job will be ours when we go to the polls. So roll up those sleeves America. I do believe it's time to do a little house cleaning.[28]

---

[28] *Union Recorder*

FIFTH GEAR

Years ago, I reached what is known as a milestone in life. This milestone was about as pleasant as a kidney stone. It hit me between the eyes and left me for dead, but SURPRISE! I SURVIVED!

The milestone I speak of is none other than my birthday. I wish I could say I reached the big 4-0, but I've been there and done that. Now I am serious as a stone... it was 5-0; half a century, five decades, over the hill. Ugh... it gives my spine the shivers to think of it! I feel younger on the inside than I look on the outside, but stiff joints and sagging body parts are daily reminders that the old gray mare ain't what she used to be. My Mom's remark "I can't believe you're that old" didn't help, but it's OK Mom, I still love you.

Old people are prone to reminisce. I recall the first few milestones in my life. I remember thinking I'd never turn 16, the "dating" age. Then it was 18, the "almost-free-to –do-whatever-I-want" age. Like all adults in training, I had all the answers; After all it was the Age of Aquarius, the enlightened '60's, and all that stuff. Then came the biggie, 21; the "drinking-voting-now-I-can-marry-without-permission" age, (California law.) I must say, THAT was a big year; because I celebrated all three.

The years following my marriage are a blur. The first 10 years passed me by faster than the cars on I-75. Sure, the speed limit decreased to 55mph, but I was stuck in first gear. I vaguely recollect something about Carter and Elvis and the price of gasoline, but the pitter-patter of 10 little feet drown out the rest of the world. We had our sixth child as the '80s dawned and this Sleeping Beauty of the '60's was replaced with a Rip Van Winkle pondering,

"Where am I?"

I thought I could slow down and casually take a look at what was going on around me. WRONG! As the decade prepared for blast off, we buckled our seat belts and braced ourselves for the terrors and expense of TEENAGERS! So, clutching our hearts and each other's hands, we shifted in to second gear and I joined the ranks of the few the proud, the working moms.

My husband and I raced through the '80's from ball practice to piano lessons and back home again. We assumed additional roles as chauffeur, coach and banker. We pinched pennies until they cried "Uncle" and robbed Peter to pay Paul for braces, instruments, and car insurance. Taking a breath, we shifted into third gear.

With toes tapping, the '90's impatiently waited for us. Pausing only to catch our breath between high school graduations and student financial aid forms, I caught my image in the mirror. "Who is that person?" I cried. There was snow on the roof top! For a short while, Lady Clairol and I became bosom buddies. But it was a surface relationship. I finally decided what you see is what you get... and more than the plot thickened.

Exhaling, we shifted in to fourth gear. We naively thought that as the offspring turned 18, we'd be able to relax a bit. WRONG AGAIN. One at a time our children left to pursue their dreams. Reluctantly, we took a back seat in their lives, watching them in the driver's seat (again) like back-seat parents, squeezing our eyes shut, trying to allow them to make their own decisions all the while holding on tightly and praying.

Dare I contemplate shifting into fifth gear? I am so tired of the back seat. I want to feel the wind in (what's left of) my hair. I want to come home and find the house exactly the way it was when I left it. I want my deodorant in my bathroom when I reach for it. I want a convertible.

A convertible! Unbelievable, the kids laugh. They think I'm too old to have a convertible. Hey, I deserve a convertible. I put the lid on the toothpaste, I get my movies back on time, and I don't put wet towels in the hamper. Besides, we've paid the price. You want to know what is unbelievable. In the last 26 years we have washed over 10,000 loads of clothes, prepared over 18,000 meals purchased two saxophones, two flutes, two trumpets, one clarinet, and one bass guitar and amplifier. We have attended over 200 various ball games, not to mention band performances, seven recitals, five proms and two senior breakfasts. We have purchased two new refrigerators, two new washers and two new freezers, as they wore out. We have spent over $129,600 on food in the last 26 years. Now THAT is unbelievable. I think if I want a convertible I should have one... but I won't it's too impractical. I must remain practical because I am preparing for the icing on the cake, the grand finale, the encore performance. I am biding my time until the grandchildren arrive.

Hehehehe, grandchildren a.k.a. "the mother's curse." I may not be willing to spoil myself, but I am looking forward to spoiling the grandchildren rotten then letting their parents deal with them when they return home. Now that will make the whole trip worthwhile.

Things could be a lot worse, you know. This old jalopy could be in the shop for repairs or worse yet, I could be stuck in REVERSE![29]

---

[29] *Union Recorder*

AT HOME ON PAGE 4A

It was suggested that I read the September 17, 1997 issue of *The Sandersville Progress*. The article of interest was <u>Food for thought</u> by Bob Garrett on page 4A. So a week later I was reading the column, my head bobbing up and downs in agreement. But there was more of interest to me on page 4A that day than just Mr. Garrett's article. As my eyes leisurely strolled across the page, I traveled from <u>Rock of Ages</u> to <u>Tom Sez</u> and <u>Out and About</u>. That day, on page 4A, I took a trip down memory lane with strangers. But you know, some of our memories are much the same, making us not strangers, but friends who have not yet met.

I am not a Southerner by birth, but a city girl raised in the Los Angeles suburbs. I married a Georgia boy, who brought me home to meet his folks. On that first trip south, he not only introduced me to his family, but also to this charming place called Georgia. In that one brief visit a flame was kindled, and it burned until we finally moved to Georgia in '73. Now I can say I'm a *Southerner by choice* and a proud one at that.

And what are my memories? Let's see. I'll start with *purple hull peas*. I remember sitting on a front porch too, but on the swing shelling purple hull peas with Mema and Papa. Sounds quaint, huh? Did I neglect to mention that it was hot as Hades, my thumb was aching and the thumbnail was about to fall off? You all can sit back and snicker, NOW, but as children I bet you hated to shell peas worse that I did as an adult. Oh, I bet I forgot one other minor detail: until 1973 I didn't even know what a purple hull pea was, and I didn't know there was so much work to getting those suckers picked and then out of the little jackets they wore. I thought peas were round and green and came out of a can. If those purple hulls didn't taste so good, I think I would have stuck with the canned ones.

His family was so patient with me. At dinner one day I wanted some more of those purple hulls, I said "pass the beans please." Forks stopped mid air in confusion. As understanding dawned, the bowl was passed. "PEAS" came the correction with a rolling of the eyes. From then on if I wasn't sure what to call it, I would just point. Ah memories…

Yep this city girl had a lot to learn. If I hadn't been loved I would have high-tailed it back to California in six months time. But we stayed and the last twenty-something years have been a roller-coaster of experiences which includes six children, but never regret.

Thank you Mr. Garrett, *the Sandersville Progress,* and the contributors to page 4A. Thank you for reminding me how glad this city girl is to be in Georgia.[30]

---

[30] *Sandersville Progress*

WHO ARE YOU?

The birth of our first grandchild has been exciting. Life that was once merely comfortable has taken on a new excitement. Our focus is now on this new young life and all she represents. She is our past and our future. And now that there is another grandchild on the way, well, we are head-over-heels in grandparent ecstasy.

This Christmas, she sat at our feet playing with her holiday bounty, temporarily distracted by the colorful toys. When the one toy she wanted was just out of her reach, she would find a way to grab it and still keep her Mommy in sight. With unsteady hands she would raise the bright gadget to eye-level, carefully examine it, and then for good measure, taste it. She is incredible. She is unique, but she is familiar. I searched her eyes and her smile to see who she looks like. I note her mannerisms and temper to see who she imitates. I catch that fleeting thoughtful look and those curious eyes and am reminded of her Daddy long ago.

She can't talk yet, but I prepare myself for the day she does. One day will she ask me who I am? What will I say to her? I am your Grandma, but I am more than that. The answer could at times be lengthy or brief, but it's always the same; I am me.[31]

---

[31] *50 +magazine* Winter 2002

WHO AM I?

I am unique, one of a kind.
I am common and I am sublime.
I am me.
I am part beauty and part beast.
I am famine I am feast.
I am me.
I am who I love and who loves me.
I am my thoughts in word and deed.
I am me.
I am every choice I'll ever make.
I am every chance I dared to take.
I am me.
I am part of a book without age.
I am just a chapter on a living page.
I am me.
I am an angel in disguise.
I am fool, yet I am wise.
I am me.
I am both fiction and fantasy.
I am a prayer on bended knee.
I am me.
I am a mirror for you to see.
I am reflection of your heredity.
I am me.
I am in you and you are in me.
We're neither the end nor the beginning you see,
For we're each a branch of a living tree.
We're not really just me,
But we.[32]

---

[32] *50's + magazine*

I'VE GOT IT, HAVE YOU?

I'm sick. At first I didn't realize I was sick, but now I'm sure of it. The strange part is I didn't know it was contagious. Well, I'm no doctor, so perhaps it isn't contagious, but never the less, I'm not the only one who has it. I'll bet you've got it too. If you're over the age of 40, my guess is you've got it and this is the time of year it is the worst.

How can you tell? Open your mouth, say "Ahhh." Hmmm. That is inconclusive. OK. Go ahead, look in the mirror. Is there a stranger looking back at you? Do you laugh at yourself when you see your reflection? Are there laugh lines around your eyes and mouth? Is there a touch of gray in your hair? Is there any hair? Do you remember what you're looking for? When you study your face, do you see your mom or dad peeking back at you around the edges? Do you remember what day it is today? If you've answered "yes" to any of the above symptoms, then, chances are, you've got it.

Oh, and you know what else? It gets worse as you age. The symptoms intensify making young folks laugh and make fun of you. It's good I guess that it's not a debilitating illness. You'll live thorough it. The best part is, there is not much pain though some of us do experience some remorse and most shed a few tears of regret. Once in a while we just plain cry for happy. When they see us the younger members of the family and friends roll their eyes and say "I'll never get that!" but they will. Just wait and see.

I must say, it's really very nice sometimes being sick. It's especially comforting to know that I'm not the only one who has it. There are even few of us who gather round the card table and discuss some of the more recent symptoms of this disease.

Is there a cure, you ask? Well, not that I know of. Besides, I don't want to be cured. This is a healthy sick. Now there's an oxymoron if I ever saw one.

So, these are the facts: if you haven't got it you will get it. When you do get it you won't want to give it up.

It's so good to sit back and relax knowing I 'm not the only one to suffer with Nostalgia.[33]

---

[33] *Union Recorder*

TREASURES

Come with me and we'll find treasures
Too rich and beautiful to measure.
Not a four-wheel drive or a hearty steed,
"The trip is short?" You cry, disappointment showing.
"Yes." You'll need only your heart
Where we are going."
Dad's strong hands, quick mind
And loyal heart
Mom's kitchen crowded with food and wisdom to impart.
Sitting at the kitchen table and reminiscing
About playing volleyball at Thanksgiving.
These simple moments and loving gestures
Will be part of your heart's best treasures.
Grandpa's stubbornness and balding head.
Grandma's piano playing and cokes in the frig.
Papa sitting on the porch just swinging
Mema's kitchen hot from the cooking and baking.
When days seem cold and you're all alone.
Bring out these treasures they'll keep you warm.
A hug, a word of praise; priceless gifts once given
From loved ones remembered
Now living in Heaven.
They're out of reach, yet, they seem so near
Because our memories keep them dear.

Our treasures, you see, are not in gold or art
Our treasures are the memories inside our heart.
Like men of old on ships a 'sailing, so Foolishly forsaking.
All for treasures for the taking
But true riches are home-made
And from us cannot be severed,
They will remain with us forever.
For these treasures of the heart are
our Soul's companions
And continue to live on with us
In heaven.
For it is written:
Where your heart is your treasure is also[34]

---

[34] Unpublished

THE LORD HAS COME

For 200 years, like a silent sentinel, this building sat quietly, sheltered in the trees. Like a grand lady watching the world go by, she waited patiently, her steeple pointing the way. Her cemetery is set apart in the trees beyond, a white picket fence supposedly separating the living from the dead. It is usually a very pretty place, but with the arrival of winter, and the shedding of leaves, it appears unkempt.

So far, I'm the only one to arrive. The hinges squeak as I slowly push open the unlocked door. Stepping in, I peer inside and confirm that the sanctuary is empty. As always, the old floor groans as I enter. It doesn't seem possible, but it is drearier and colder inside than it is outside. The clatter of the closing door echoes in the stillness causing goose bumps to tickle my spine. Quickly, I flick on the lights.

The sun has been up for hours, it is hidden behind gray clouds. The only thing comforting is the cross glowing softly on the wall. I quickly make my way to the thermostats behind the pulpit. With shivering fingers I adjust the temperature on each then wait to hear the units kick in. Satisfied I pick up a bulletin and start back to sit in my usual spot on the third pew. Seated, I glance at my watch. It is 9:55 a.m. I wonder if anyone will show up this Christmas Eve.

The thought of the holidays draws my attention to the Christmas tree. Though it is beginning to dry out and sag around the edges, it is still beautiful. It is perfectly shaped and dressed in white and gold glittering religious ornaments. An angel in flowing white robes crowns the treetop. If I didn't know any better, I'd think she was gazing directly at me. The two lovely wreaths on the Sunday school room doors were made by Frances and together with the grand poinsettia at the altar, create a lovely picture of Christmas.

The room is beginning to warm up. I take off my gloves and stand to loosen the zipper on my jacket. I turn at the subtle sound of a decoration falling off the tree. Laying down my gloves, I walk over to pick it up. It is a small cross stitched ornament bearing a familiar name.

Thoughtfully, I place it back on the tree. These ornaments are a delicious mystery. Every year "someone" makes one for every new person in the church. Next to the ornament is another with an equally familiar name. And next to that one, is mine. I remove it from the tree.

Only a few short weeks ago we crowded around this tree to hang these handmade delicacies.

As Emily played *Jesus loves me,* the church family placed each on the tree under the watchful eyes of the angel and possibly of that mysterious someone. That day was a cold and dreary day too, but there was enough light shining through the stained glass to illuminate the names of those who have gone to sleep in Christ. For one brief moment, we were all together, celebrating the first Advent of the Christ child.

Returning to my pew I continue to wait. Nervous now, I constantly glance at my watch. It is 10:30 a.m. And no one has arrived. Why am I surprised? It's what I expected. My heart is heavy, but the small hand-made ornament is light in my hands. With my fingers I trace the letters of my name. I guess I'll never know who made it.

Looking back at the Christmas tree I study for the first time the different symbols known as Christmons. All of them reflect the Christ in some form or fashion. Come to think about it, the names on the tree each reflect Christ as well.

To keep from fidgeting, I walk back to the tree to study it more closely, looking for answers. Both the living and the dead adorn this tree. As I read each name aloud I visualize each face and each smile. At first, I am tempted to remember their flaws, but I refuse. Instead I dwell on a kindness, a compliment, a hug or an offer for prayer. With each ornament memories like instant replays, flash through my mind. This one was in the choir and that one mowed the grass. One memory snowballs into another until I recall vividly other things like: solemn moments at communion, the excitement of Vacation Bible School, Homecoming and revival.

I am ashamed when I remember that IF I came to church, I generally day-dreamed through Brother Bill's sermons. I wonder if he ever noticed I was the first one out the door. During Children's Sermon it was difficult for me to smile as children squirmed and laughed on the floor. I was as equally puzzled at the smiles of proud parents and grandparents. Like a raging flood, I recall my own times of joy and sorrow and those who helped me through my tough times with a hug or a card. Sadly, what I do remember most, is that I always kept myself on the outside looking in. it doesn't matter now. The waiting is over. Tomorrow is Christmas, but last night, without lights, music and fanfare, the Christ came.

It is nearly 11:00 a.m. sitting back down in my pew I try to ignore the fact that only the building remains; the building and the things inside it, including me. I am afraid. It is warm inside the church now, but I'm trembling. Next to me a tattered Bible lies forgotten. It has fallen open to the last page. The former owner has highlighted the last two verses, "He who testifies to these things says, 'Yes, I am coming quickly...'" I slam closed the book and shove it away.

Hopelessly, I ache for the sight of a familiar face, a welcoming smile and one of Phil's bear hugs. Tears run freely down my cheeks. Fidgeting, I reach for a hymnal and the book falls open... *Amazing Grace how sweet the sound that saved a wretch like me.* My bulletin slides from my lap, fluttering to the floor, with it a special insert *The Lord Has Come!* Picking up the errant pages I shove them into the hymnal. Abstractedly, I flip the pages ... *Do you know my Jesus?* My eyes blur. I turn them faster... *Just as I am without one plea... Great is thy faithfulness... It is well with my soul.* Sobbing I toss the book away.

It's true! I came here this morning to be sure. Oh God! I've missed it! I swallow the panic rising in my throat. I cling to the pew in front of me until my knuckles turn white. My eyes dart around the empty room.

How could I miss it? All around me there were signs! The tree and its decoration, the hymnals, the Sunday school lessons, the people, the weekly message, the cross...

Ignoring the distant sound of a closing door, I hurry down the aisle to kneel at the altar. Looking up I see only the cross and the gentle light beyond. The words want to stick in my throat, but I manage to whisper them anyway.

"Oh, God! Is it too late for me?"[35]

---

[35] (To the body of Christ at Montpelier Church, Keep the Faith!, 2000) Unpublished

FLASHBACK

Walking into the living room, I glanced at the television program blaring into the empty space. I walk over to shut it off. What was that? Quickly, I turn the set back on. It can't be, I argue silently with myself. I stare dumbly at the screen as ancient memories are resurrected before my very eyes!

I hold my head in disbelief. It's a flash back. I 'm re-living my childhood years again. Scenes from my adolescence flicker before my closed eyes, triggering a string of memories from long ago... braided hair, guitars, the Mamas and the Papas ... foolish days as a flower-child wannabe.

A kaleidoscope of images crowds my mind. The images start out in black and white: Leave it to Beaver, Rin Tin Tin, Superman and Dr. Kildare. They laugh at me as they all dance together in my head. What's happening? Am I dying? Opening my eyes I try to shake it loose and come back to reality.

The noise and commotion from the TV bring my eyes back to focus once more on the screen. Bumps and thumps, yelling and hitting, it is all so grotesque. I feel my body tremble as chill bumps run up and down my spine. No! It can't be! This is too much! I click the set off and spin around.

Furtively, I check around the corners of the adjoining rooms. Good no one saw this, it would be too embarrassing. I still can't believe it... I thought it was over, gone, a thing of the past. It was bad enough the first time. How many others know it's back? Aghh! I thought those memories were neatly tucked away in the closets of my mind between the forgotten folk songs and my long lost naiveté. But NO, my worst fears have become reality!

I must be sure. Dare I look again? I slip quietly back into the living room and click on the television set once again, making sure the sound is turned down lest anyone hear. Oh no! It's still there and it hasn't changed a bit, it has a new name and a slightly different look, but it's still the same. My shoulders droop as I shake my head. A tear trickles down my cheek when I realize I am doomed.

There is nothing I can do about it. I'll just have to learn to live with it AGAIN. In stubborn defiance, I raise my head high and square my shoulders. I refuse to be a part of it. I'll just ignore it. I walk away in stoic silence with a vow on my lips. I just DARE someone in this house to turn on Roller Jam![36]

---

[36] *Union Recorder*

MEATLOAF FOR SUPPER

As usual, I am up ahead of everyone. I'm still tired. Standing in the kitchen I survey the damage. There are glasses and odd dishes to wash from the evening before. The table needs to be wiped and the floor swept. When that is finished, I need to mix the meat loaf then wash and wrap the baking potatoes. Sigh.

Reluctantly, I clean out the drainer then run water in the sink to begin washing dishes. As I work, I intentionally make a ruckus, hoping to wake them all up. I fantasize them running out and offering to help. Who am I kidding? Grumbling, I finish the dishes, wipe up the counter then put on the coffee. It doesn't take a genius to figure out why I am upset. They are sleeping in on this beautiful Sunday morning and I am working.

Grabbing the broom I start to sweep, shuffling bits of sand half way across the room. I am wondering how the floor can get so dirty. As I sweep, I turn my attention toward heaven to complain about my uncaring family, but a sudden thought stops me. There is something about this Sunday scenario that seems vaguely familiar. Like an instant replay I see it: the familiar Mary-Martha syndrome.

It's funny. Whenever I think about Mary and Martha I always imagine that I am the gentle attentive Mary not the moody anxious Martha. Putting the broom away, I picture it in my mind. Yes, yes, see? There I am, sitting at his feet hanging on his every word, while that mean old Martha is crabbing in the back ground! Wait a minute! Who am I kidding? Today I am no less than a moody, moaning Martha.

Absentmindedly, I set the place mats on the table. WHAT am I doing? Isn't this a Sunday supper as usual? The question is obvious: WHY am I doing the Sunday supper thing? Am I doing it because I want to or because I think I'm supposed to? Hmm. If this is what I really want to do then it shouldn't be a chore, but a joyful offering, MY offering, not theirs.

Walking in to the kitchen I toss the meat, oatmeal, eggs and seasoning in the bowl and start mixing. Meatloaf. Who eats meatloaf on a Sunday, for heaven sake? It's my fault. I didn't get to the store yesterday and meatloaf is all I have to offer. Now, I'm feeling guilty.

"What's wrong with me? I'm confused. Lord, I love my family."

"So did Martha," He replies. "And Martha loved ME."

Whoa! I have never stopped to think about that. Martha, Loved Jesus just like Mary loved him? What happened? Was it wrong to prepare a meal for Jesus? Was it wrong to want Him to have the best? Could it be that Martha wanted to be with the others listening to Jesus rather than working? Was she fixing her meatloaf out of obligation? After all, how would it look not to feed Him or the guests? Did her keen sense of obligation overpower the needs of her heart?

Placing the meatloaf in a baking dish, I enter a guess. Since she complained, she must have been doing it out of obligation, wanting all the while to be sitting with Mary and the others; or in my case, sleeping in the bed.

The meatloaf and potatoes are now in the cold oven. I'll turn on the oven as we walk out the door for church. Washing my hands at the sink, I wonder. Would Martha's family have noticed if the place mats weren't out? Would they have been upset if they had sandwiches and chips for dinner rather than meatloaf and baked potatoes? Would they have been content with whatever she provided and happy just to have her sitting with them as they listened to Jesus?

I have to chuckle. For me to have a good day or a bad day depends not so much on which side of the bed I get up on, but rather, with whom I chose to walk into my day and what a day this has already been.

I recognize that at certain times in my life I've acted like a doubting Thomas, an arrogant Peter, or a faithful John. Sometimes I've even acted like the martyr Paul.

The truth is, I'm all of them. That's the beauty of the scripture - it's full of virtue and villainy – just like me. I am a Thomas growing into a Paul – I am Martha learning when to be a Mary – I am me learning to be Jesus.

I am finished and feeling better. I hear my husband banging around in the bathroom now, getting ready for church. I pour us each a cup of coffee before leaving the kitchen to join him. Yes. There will probably be a Sunday supper next week, but I'm not going to guarantee what it will be. I guess it depends on who will be cooking: Mary or Martha?[37]

---

[37] Unpublished

OMA SAYS

Don't tell anyone ... but I'm getting old. I know this not because of the gray-headed stranger staring at me from the mirror in my bathroom, but because I can see myself aging in the changing faces of our children. The older I get, the older they get! And the older I get the faster time flies; each year quickly becoming a colorful blur. It seems that before I can throw up my hand to say "Hi" to a new year, it's time to say "bye." This whole aging thing would be really tough for me if it weren't for the grandchildren.

Our granddaughter had barely turned one this year when our grandson arrived with a bang on the 4th of July. I was asked, "Is he pretty?" of course he is! I've never had an ugly grandchild, have you? Of course not! Each one is beautiful; a miracle in a baggy birthday suit; sleepy-eyed and soft as silk; Oma's fountain of youth. One look at one of those precious faces and I'm ready to face what lies ahead.

For one of the baby showers, we were asked to contribute a scrapbook. You know, leave a legacy for the new parents; pearls of wisdom, wise counsel. Never at a loss for words, the following is the "gem" I offered.

Dear Ethan,
Here are a few words of wisdom I'd like to share with you as you begin your life as a child. It was tough enough getting here, but ahead of you lays an even more difficult assignment: raising your parents. Being the first child, you will have the task of breaking in the new Mom and Dad and

training them for your siblings to follow. This is an awesome job. Here are a few things for you to remember:

Love is always patient and kind.

In the beginning parents sometimes make mistakes or seem unsure of themselves. They are after all, new at this. Your patience will be needed until they get the hang of parenting. Just smile at them a lot and make cute little noises. Laughing and giggling will also reassure them that you love them even when they make mistakes.

Parents' become keenly aware of other children after they have one of their own. They will even hold other children, but don't worry. This is how they discover there is no other child as sweet and lovable as you. Before I forget, there will also be times when they make a big fuss over the dog, Murphy, and even seem to ignore you. This doesn't mean they don't love you; they just don't want Murphy to have her feelings hurt. You will always be top dog.

Love is not boastful or conceited, it is never rude and never seeks its own advantage, it does not take offense or store up grievances.

There will be times, Ethan that you will want to play with Mom and Dad or just be held and they will be too busy with adult stuff to even notice. This will make you want to scream at them and stomp your feet just to get their attention. You might feel like hitting someone or pulling hair, but be brave. Remember, they are only parents and they have much to learn.

Love does not rejoice at wrong doing, but finds its joy in the truth.

There will be times when you feel forgotten. They may even leave you for a while with strangers making you feel like you've been abandoned, but rest assured, they will be back because you are their heart. You will have to forgive them too when they are too slow to see that you have a tummy ache, or that a new tooth is bothering you, or that you have another diaper rash.

Always remember that even if they sometimes don't show it, they love you.

Love is always ready to make allowances, to trust, to hope and to endure whatever comes.

As you grow older Ethan, you will think your parents have lost their minds. They will make you do things like homework and chores. They will set boundaries for you that will all seem totally unrealistic. It will be during times like these that you will have to trust them. Trust them to know what is best for you because they have been where you will be. Trust them because they would rather die than have anything happen to you.

Besides, you can put up with almost anything until you are grown up enough to be on your own.

Love never comes to an end.

Listen closely, this is most important. When you are older, you will hide from your Mom and Dad's love. You will leave their home to be on your own and to find your place in this big, exciting world.

You will change as you grow older. You will learn to make your own decisions. You will learn as we all did one mistake at a time. Then one day it will occur to you that Mom and Dad weren't so dumb after all.

One day it will dawn on you how much they love you. Let me tell you a secret ... you will never out grow the need for your Mom and Dad's love. Even when you are grown, their love will be like a Band-Aid. Everyone knows you don't need a Band-Aid all the time, just when life gives you a boo boo.

Well, that is all I have to say, Ethan. These are not my words, but the Words of your Heavenly Father.

"As it is written, these remain: faith, hope and love ... and the greatest of these is love."

It is no secret; if you have love you have everything. Rest assured, Ethan, you have it all.

Love, Oma, 1 Cor. 13:4-8a, 13[38]

---

[38] *50's + Magazine*

ARE WE ALMOST THERE?

As a child, I looked forward to summer vacation and camping in the mountains. Mom spent a week packing up the camping gear, food and assorted paraphernalia. On Saturday, Dad would somehow load it all into the car along with his fishing gear and the dog. Then my parents, my little brother and I would squeeze in and head for the mountains. We would barely be out of the city limits before my brother would impatiently ask, "Are we almost there?"

Their response, "No, not yet, but it won't be long now." And that would satisfy my brother for awhile.

As the hours passed, we would dream aloud, "Hope the lake is high?"

"Hope the fishing is good!"

"Hope we can get that good camp site nearest the outhouse!" and so forth.

We fairly itched to be there. Our excitement grew with every mile. Just think, a whole week of hot dogs, hamburgers, chips and colas, and all the swimming in the lake a body could stand! Maybe this year I'd even dive off the *big rock!* And the bonus; there was a movie shown outdoors every Friday night!

Yes, I was excited too, but I knew better than to ask a hundred times, "Are we there yet?" By the time we got to the camp grounds, my folks were down to their last nerve. Opening the car doors, we would all fall out and make a beeline for our first glimpse of the lake. Even the dog was excited, barking and running with us. Topping the hill we would see the lake, shimmering in the sun. Excited beyond belief, we'd return to the car to quickly unload and set up camp. In record time we'd have the tent up and our clothes changed. Then we'd take off for the water with snorkel, fins, and towels in tow. Dad would be close behind dragging his fishing pole and bait and mom would just bring her sunglasses, a folding chair and a good book. This was the life. This is what we looked forward to all year. The hardest part of waiting for summer vacation was the actual trip to the lake. It was the hardest part simply because we were almost there.

Allow me to digress. I had a dream the other night. I dreamt a doctor told me I was dying. Then I woke up. What a shocking thought! I dwelt on it awhile, pondering my feelings. And you know what I concluded? Life is like a Star Trek movie. We slip into our environmentally approved space suit, strap on our polyurethane stereo head gear and step into our lives. Then we move through each day at *warp speed*. Everything around us is a blur; whether it be good or bad. Only when we hear the big **"D"** word do we slow down and take a good look around ourselves. Suddenly, what was a confusing becomes understood; what was lost is found; and what was cheap is now priceless.

But you know what? We are all dying. From the day we take our first breath, we begin that journey toward death. It is unavoidable. It **is** coming; we just don't know **when** each of us will cross over into the great beyond. So why do we hate the thought of dying? Perhaps it's because unlike summer vacation, we don't have the slightest inkling where we are going or what awaits us. I know what waits for me. It is more exciting than a thousand summer vacations. It is more beautiful than all the wonders of the world. It is more refreshing than a long swallow of ice water on a scorching day. The mere thought of it is enough to make me dance and sing and laugh and cry all at the same time. It is my treasured hope and my lasting joy. It is what I see beyond the clouds and through the sunbeams. It is what keeps my heart from breaking when I see what goes on around me.

I can hardly wait! "Are we almost there?"

And Jesus says, "It won't be long now."

1 Corinthians 2:9 But as it is written, Eye hath not seen, nor ear heard, neither have entered into the heart of man, the things which God hath prepared for them that love him. KJV[39]

---

[39] *Outreach*

THE DOGWOOD

It's usually not my task, but since no one else was home, I walked up to the mailbox today. The sky was clear blue, the breeze gentle and the sun warm. I paused to enjoy the moment, taking time to notice the obvious signs of spring all around me. Thinking my mission accomplished, I turned back toward the house. That is when she caught my eye. I hadn't noticed her in ages, so I was surprised how tall and beautiful she had grown.

I remember her from a dozen years ago, when she was less mature, with so much growth ahead of her. I vividly recall eight rambunctious children squeezing beside her to have their picture taken, each dressed in their Easter finery. I still have that picture. Back then, the children were nearly as tall as she, but like the children, she has grown.

Today I delight in her beauty, slender limbs and long graceful fingers reaching heavenward. She reminds me of a beautiful ballerina, pirouetting in the breeze. She is the picture of peace and tranquility. She nearly floats before my eyes in her lovely white Easter gown. The mere sight of her is a gift in itself. Yet, there is just a hint of sorrow...

It is said that long ago the Dogwood was a very large tree and because of this was used to construct the cross of Christ. Because she felt such horror on this account, Christ promised the Dogwood she would never again grow large enough to be put to such use. As a memorial of Christ's passion, her blossoms now grow in the shape of a cross, the petals bear brown and red nail prints, and a crown of thorns grace the center of her flower. Thus at Easter time, her glory declares His Glory.

I stand by the mailbox, enjoying the moment, but in the back of my mind I know this lovely spring offering will soon vanish, though only briefly. In the blinking of an eye, it will be replaced by a profusion of lively green leaves. This is yet another testimony to the Giver of Life.

I start back with the mail, my mind wandering ahead. It is written, *to everything there is a time and a season.* The air will turn crisp and cold as creation prepares to rest, but the testimony of the Dogwood will continue. When the world around her appears dead and colorless, she will be clothed in brilliant reds, reminiscent of the blood of Christ. And at last, when winter has come to stay, her burden will be lifted and she too will rest and wait in silence. And should her Redeemer tarry, come springtime she will gladly begin again her colorful testimony to His Glory and Grace.

Blessed be the King that cometh in the name of the Lord: peace in heaven and glory in the highest. And some of the Pharisees from among the multitude said unto him, "Master, rebuke thy disciples!" And He answered and said unto them, "I tell you that if these should hold their peace, the stones would immediately cry out." Luke 19:38-40

Sing, O ye heavens; for the Lord hath done it: shout, ye lower parts of the earth: break forth into singing, ye mountains; O forest, and every tree therein, for the Lord hath redeemed Jacob and glorified Himself in Israel. Isaiah 44:23[40]

---

[40] *Union Recorder*

GRACE

The preacher spoke of the zealot, Saul, who passionately and adamantly hated the faithless Jews-now Christians. These new Christians were traitors to the faith. They were heretics. They followed this new religion and shamefully forgot the great IAM, the commandments and the prophets.

But, Saul was a devout man. He was a learned man. He loved the law and the traditions. Anger and rage coursed through his veins at the very thought of those Christians. In the name of this Jesus, they committed violations of untold proportions, mocking everything sacred to him and to all Jewish people. They had to be stopped. So he hunted them down like dogs, rejoicing in their punishment, and basking in the glory. He did it for God.

He did it for God! What a thought! Such vehemence! He would extract revenge. He would see that justice reigned. And he was good at it, very good. The mere mention of his name brought goose bumps to the flesh of all the believers, but even Saul of Tarsus could not stop all of them. He could squelch a flicker here and there, but the flaming name of Jesus spread like wild fire throughout Israel.

God's grace.

Then came the light and the voice like thunder.

"SAUL, WHY DO YOU PERSECUTE ME?"

Reeling from the blinding flash, the great Saul falls from his mighty place, hitting the rocky ground. Crying out in confusion, the dazed horse dances about him in fear, filling the air with noise and confusion. Looking up toward the sun, Saul gropes in the sudden darkness. What had been plain as day became dark as Egypt. He struggles to stand, reaching for something with which to balance himself and falls again. Great droplets of sweat mingled with tears leave wet trails as they ran down his dusty face. Struggling to his feet, he fearfully cries aloud,

"Who are you? WHO ARE YOU?"

The thunderous response, **"I AM JESUS, WHOM YOU ARE PERSECUTING."**

And Saul falls back.

Marvelous grace.

For three days Saul remained in the belly of his whale. He had met the great IAM and lived to tell it. For three days those deafening words rang in his ears and reverberated throughout his entire body.

"I AM - JESUS, WHOM YOU ARE PERSECUTING.. I AM - JESUS, WHOM YOU ARE PERSECUTING.. I AM - JESUS, WHOM YOU ARE PERSECUTING."

From deep in his soul, Saul of Tarsus cries and pleads with God. He fasts and prays. His body aches, his eyes are swollen and his voice is hoarse. Every muscle in his body groans. His heart breaks. After three days, Saul dies.

Grace that is greater than all my sin. He who is forgiven much loves much.

After three days, Paul is born.

Leave me not O precious Savior. I too am such a sinner. I rebel against your word and at times wrestle vehemently with your Holy spirit within me. I hinder the work of your *body* with my disobedience, absence and procrastination. I fail to pray for those who serve you and are persecuted for your name's sake. I am blind to the consequences of my actions until I too hear...

"I AM JESUS, WHOM YOU ARE PERSECUTING."

Forgive me.

Amazing grace, how sweet the sound that saved a wretch like me. I once was lost but now I'm found. I was blind...but now...I see.[41]

---

[41] *Mustard Seed*

JESUS KNOWS

1 Cor. 9:22
To the weak I became weak to win the weak. I have
Become all things to all men so that by
All possible means I might save some.

Whenever I experienced problems or whenever I tried to give comfort or encouragement to someone whose life was in turmoil and confusion, I offered platitudes like:

"Jesus understands, He's been there." or "Jesus feels your pain, He hurt too."

But even as I spoke the only words I believed should bring comfort, I harbored my own doubts.

Jesus is God - How can He feel what I feel? How can the creator feel something so small as the pain of my arthritis. How can He know the helpless agony of watching a child make all the wrong choices? How can He know how I feel about a lot of things? He wasn't married. He didn't have a family? He isn't me. HOW can He know?"

"Ok. Here's the plan." The coach paces back and to in front of me.

"See this odd-shaped, little ball? All you have to do is carry it down the field and across that line." It's a big field, but that sounds easy enough. I think this could be fun. I love games.

"Oh, and you know what? You will have help. There will be ten other people just like yourself, to help you carry this little ball down the field and over the line."

Wow. How easy can it be? But wait, what is the coach saying now...

"Of course, there are rules and regulations about how this is to be accomplished and there's just one or two other little things you need to know; there will be eleven other people on the field who DON'T want you to carry this ball down the field. They will be doing everything they can to push you back, away from your goal and knock you off your feet. Not only that, they will try to tear the ball away from you and incapacitate you."

Gulp. Now I see why I need ten other people to help me.

"But don't worry. I'll be on the side lines giving you instructions. I'll help you. I have lots of ways to get this ball down the field and over the goal line. Just keep your eyes on me."

Now, what if you were asked to quarterback this NFL team, but you are just a little boy? Well that would be unfair. You'd be sure to lose. You would be lacking experience, and ability to fight the opponent. They'd destroy you.

Well, let's reverse it. WHAT IF You were an NFL quarterback on a little league team of 12 year-olds. This would be equally unfair. His team wouldn't have to work; he'd just pick up the ball and run with it. He would have no need for a team and he'd be too big to stop.

Hmm. Well, how about this. We take Joe Montana's know how, experience, and ability and squeeze all that into a little boys body. This little boy would be no one particularly special. Just an average little kid, and he would quarterback the little league team made up of his physical peers. Would that work? It would be a fair physical contest, yes. This quarterback would know from experience what to do and when to do it. But, he would also be handicapped. His handicap would be his body. He would have to struggle against the limitations of this little boy body, just like the other players on both teams.

It's not just the individual experiences that allow Jesus to be so compassionate, it is the fact that he played the game with the same rules and under the same limitations that we have to play the game by. He willingly made that choice. Imagine all that glory, wisdom and power restrained in time and inside a piece of flesh. In fact, it's like all the wisdom of the ages compressed into a thimble; the power of a hurricane contained in a paper bag; the glory of a thousand suns restricted to a single night light. Impossible? Not for God. HE became handicapped to show us that we can overcome. He believed He could do it so He put "feet" to His faith and walked through this life. He became the victor and we, the prize. He walked this earth the same way we have to, so that we could follow in those victorious footsteps all the way. to Heaven.[42]KJV

---

[42] Unpublished

HE IS

Because He loves me
He is
My hiding place when I cannot face life
Because He loves me
He is
My strength when I am too weak to go on
Because He loves me
He is
My chastiser when I submit to anger
Because He loves me
He is
My savior when I fear I will sink
Because He loves me
He is
My friend when I think I'm alone
Because He loves me
He is
My hope when I don't want to go on
Because He loves me
My comfort when I have been broken
Because He loves me
He is
Silent when I'm too busy to listen
Because He loves me

He is

Patient with me when I forget about Him

Because He loves me

He is

There to touch me when I least expect it

Because He loves me

He is

My shield when I hold Him up

Because He loves me

He is

My Lord even when I don't put Him first

Because He loves me

He is

My God when I remember who HE is

And only

Because He loves me

Can I do all things. [43]

---

[43] *The Mustard Seed*